YORK TRAMWAYS AND TROLLEYBUSES

Barry M Marsden

Series editor Robert J Harley

MP Middleton Press

Cover picture: Details are given in caption 40. The colours represent the bright blue and ivory of the livery of York Corporation Tramways.

Published July 2006

ISBN 1 904474 82 9

© Middleton Press, 2006

Design Deborah Esher

Published by
        Middleton Press
        Easebourne Lane
        Midhurst, West Sussex
        GU29 9AZ
Tel: 01730 813169
Fax: 01730 812601
Email: info@middletonpress.co.uk
www.middletonpress.co.uk

Printed & bound by Biddles Ltd, Kings Lynn

CONTENTS

HORSE AND ELECTRIC CARS

TROLLEYBUSES

INTRODUCTION AND ACKNOWLEDGEMENTS

York is one of my favourite cities, and one I have visited many times. It is in many ways a 'classic' example of early urban passenger transport, having hosted horse trams, electric trams, trolleybuses and motorbuses, though its narrow medieval streets must have caused many problems with constructing and maintaining the appropriate track and overhead for equine and electric vehicles. The privately-run horse tramway was only a minor undertaking, with a route length of 2.75 miles/4.4 km serviced by some 15 cars, and struggling for viability throughout its short life, but the electric tramway, a corporation enterprise, was more successful. It covered some 8.5 miles/13.6 km and ran over 40 open top vehicles. In plan the system was a radial one, with various arms spreading outwards from the central railway station, which was the hub of the whole network. A mini trolleybus line was opened after World War I as a cheaper supplement to the existing tramway. It only operated on one single route, and enjoyed two separate short lives, but at most only used four railless vehicles.

The photographs which illustrate this album come from a variety of sources, many originating as commercial postcards, though a number of individual images are also included. For assistance with pictures, reference material and identifications I am indebted to Bradford Reference Library, York Local Studies Library, Stanley King, Robin Symonds, Colin Routh, James Leslie and Norman Blount. I am particularly grateful to the City of York Council for permission to use copyright images from their collection (City of York Council www.imagineyork.co.uk). My special thanks are due to Terry Russell who produced an excellent car drawing.

GEOGRAPHICAL SETTING

The City of York was founded by the IX Hispanic Legion as a forward supply base during the subjugation of the Brigantes by the Romans in the early 70s AD, at the highest navigable point of the River Ouse where it meets the River Foss. Eboracum rapidly developed as a military and trading centre, becoming a walled civitas capital, and the second town in the province of Britannia. Emperor Septimius Severus died there in 211 AD, and in 306 Constantine was proclaimed emperor in the city. The Northumbrian Angles reoccupied the site in the early 7th century, naming it Eorwic, and the Viking host captured the city in 866; it flourished under their control as Jorvik.

York has always been important as a defensive, market, ecclesiastical and transport centre, and these aspects are emphasised by the well-preserved walls, the famous minster, the open-air market and the railway station. Several prominent museums thrive within the city, including the Railway Museum, the Castle Museum, the Yorkshire Museum and the Jorvik Viking Centre.

HISTORICAL BACKGROUND

The first York tramway was inaugurated in 1879 with the construction of a 4ft/1219mm gauge line running from the Plough Inn at Fulford north to Fishergate, which opened on 27th February 1880, with a depot at Fulford Cross. The original rolling stock included three single-deck Starbuck horse trams, in a chocolate and white livery, and a Perrett double-deck combined steam car (some accounts refer to two examples), though the latter conveyance was speedily returned to its makers after the initial trials. On 29th July 1882 the line was extended westward through the city centre via Tower Street, Clifford Street, Micklegate, Blossom Street and The Mount, as far as Mount Vale, Knavesmire. A short branch was constructed from the end of Bridge Street into Station Road to serve the NER Station, though this spur closed four years later. Both lines were single-track, apart from a short double length in Clifford Street.

Two more cars were ordered after the 1882 extension, but were discarded in favour of five single-deckers, again probably from Starbuck. In 1885 the owners, the York Tramways Company, were taken over by Imperial Tramways and from 1st January 1886 the line was operated by a subsidiary, the City of York Tramways Company. In 1890 seven of the cars had upper deck seating added, and in 1903 five second-hand trams, all two-deckers, were purchased as replacements for five time-expired vehicles. By the early 20th century, disputes between the company and the corporation over the condition of the track were becoming frequent, and on 27th February 1909 the latter purchased the undertaking, operating the facility themselves whilst working on the electrification and expansion of the line.

Work commenced on converting and extending the old horse tramway on 1st September 1909, just before the line closed on the 7th of that month. The first electric car service, the rebuilt two-mile Fulford-Nessgate part of the old track, began on 20th January 1910, now operating on a 3ft 6in./1067mm gauge, after an opening ceremony in which Mayor James Birch took the controls of decorated Car 1. The Fulford Cross depot was enlarged to house the 18 Brush open-toppers which were delivered in batches in a royal blue and cream livery. They were mounted on Brush long wheelbase (8ft. 6in./2590mm) trucks. A water car (No.19) was also provided, which was identical to a vehicle furnished for the Chesterfield Corporation Tramways in 1909, and designed by the Chesterfield manager, Robert Acland.

The whole network was designed as a radial system with all lines spreading out into the suburbs from the railway station which acted as the central pivot. Over the next few years routes opened south to South Bank, south-west to Dringhouses, west to Acomb, north to Haxby and east to Hull Road. The second line, which opened on 17th March, ran from Nessgate, crossing the river by the Ouse Bridge and extending via The Mount to Dringhouses on Tadcaster Road. A short spur ran west off Blossom Street to the railway bridge on Holgate Road. This line was then extended to Acomb on 19th June, using two cars based at a temporary depot at Acomb; passengers from Acomb had to disembark and cross Holgate Bridge until 1st August 1911, whilst it was being rebuilt. On 9th June 1910 a northern branch was opened, running from the station across Lendal Bridge out as far as Haxby Road. In January 1916 the terminus at Rose Street was extended some 200 yards further north as far as the Rowntree Cocoa Works for the benefit of the Rowntree workforce. In 1911 three more Brush cars (20-23), were added to the fleet, followed by Nos. 24-27 the following year.

On 30th July 1913, a southern route was opened to South Bank via Nunnery Lane and Bishopthorpe Road. Four more Brush open-toppers (28-31) were ordered, the first vestibuled cars in service, but were insufficient to meet passenger demand, and in 1914 four trailer cars (32-35) were purchased for use at peak periods. It seems however that the 25hp motors of the trams were not powerful enough to haul fully loaded cars and trailers on route gradients, and the latter languished in the depot until Brush trams, cars 36-41, arrived in 1916-17 with more potent 35hp motors.

The radial network, which was mostly double track, was completed on 14th June 1916, with the opening of an eastern route from Nessgate along Walmgate to the quaintly-named Bee's Wing Hotel on Hull Road. In 1925 a state-of-the-art English Electric single-deck one-man demi-car entered service as No.37, after the tram fleet had been renumbered. In this revamping, cars 20-31 became 19-30 and 36-41 became 31-36. Presumably by this time the water car and the trailers had been withdrawn. In 1929 the corporation built two of their own open-top cars, 37-38, using two trailer bodies, a spare truck and a further truck from the redundant water car. EE car 37, which had proved unpopular in service, was cut down to serve as an un-numbered sand/salt wagon. That same year three ex-Wolverhampton balcony cars (39-41) joined the undertaking, after their top covers were removed, and in 1930 Nos 42-45, ex Burton-on-Trent balcony cars became the last trams to join the fleet, again after the dismantling of their roofs. In 1931 all vehicles were given a new paint scheme, in 'bright' blue and ivory, a design which increased the blue at the expense of the old white.

By this time the service was running at a loss, and the corporation made the decision to replace the trams with motorbuses. On 1st April 1934 they set up a Joint Committee with the Yorkshire Road Car Company to facilitate this policy with their shared bus fleets. On 6th January 1935 the Dringhouses branch was abandoned, and less than a year later, on 16th November 1935, the remainder of the network followed suit. The last official car, No.1, was ironically the same conveyance that had opened the system some 25 years before.

In 1914, the corporation had obtained powers to operate trolley vehicles on four routes, as supplements to the existing tramways. Due to the war the scheme was delayed until 1920, and only one route was completed, a 1.25 mile/2 km stretch from Pavement north-east to Heworth, which opened on 22nd December 1920 with four single-deck Railless cars numbered 6-9 (though one source gives the numbers as 7-10). Hopes were that a municipal housing estate under construction near Heworth terminus would stimulate local traffic revenue when it was completed.

The four trackless were reshod with pneumatic tyres in 1925, but abandonment of the branch was being mooted as early as 1927, and on 31st December 1929 the mini-service was discontinued, and the trolleybuses replaced by petrol vehicles. However the corporation had a subsequent change of heart, and the overhead was remodelled and realigned to permit higher speeds, and a Doncaster double-decker, Karrier E6 No.22, was tried out on the line. It proved unsuitable for the narrow, twisting streets, and three state-of-the-art Karrier-Clough E4 single-deckers (Nos. 30-32) were ordered, to service the route, in the same smart livery as the later tramcar style.

An extension to the Fulford Cross depot allowed the three trolleybuses to be garaged there, and a single set of wires ran from the depot to the Pavement turning loop to give the vehicles access to and from the garage. The distance involved was almost equal to the Heworth route itself! Sadly, the second York trolleybus era was almost as short as the first. In 1934 York Corporation and the West Yorkshire Road Car Company agreed to liquidate York Corporation Transport in favour of a new York/West Yorkshire organisation, and the trackless cars ceased operation on 5th January 1935. The three Karriers found a new home in Chesterfield as their Nos. 18-20, but their respite was short-lived. After some 27 months the Chesterfield system also closed, and the vehicles were duly scrapped.

HORSE AND ELECTRIC TRAMCARS

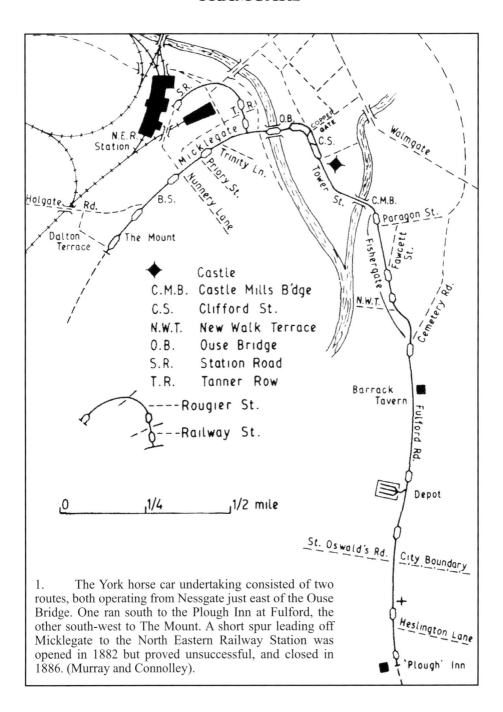

Castle
C.M.B. Castle Mills B'dge
C.S. Clifford St.
N.W.T. New Walk Terrace
O.B. Ouse Bridge
S.R. Station Road
T.R. Tanner Row

----Rougier St.

----Railway St.

0   1/4   1/2 mile

1.   The York horse car undertaking consisted of two routes, both operating from Nessgate just east of the Ouse Bridge. One ran south to the Plough Inn at Fulford, the other south-west to The Mount. A short spur leading off Micklegate to the North Eastern Railway Station was opened in 1882 but proved unsuccessful, and closed in 1886. (Murray and Connolley).

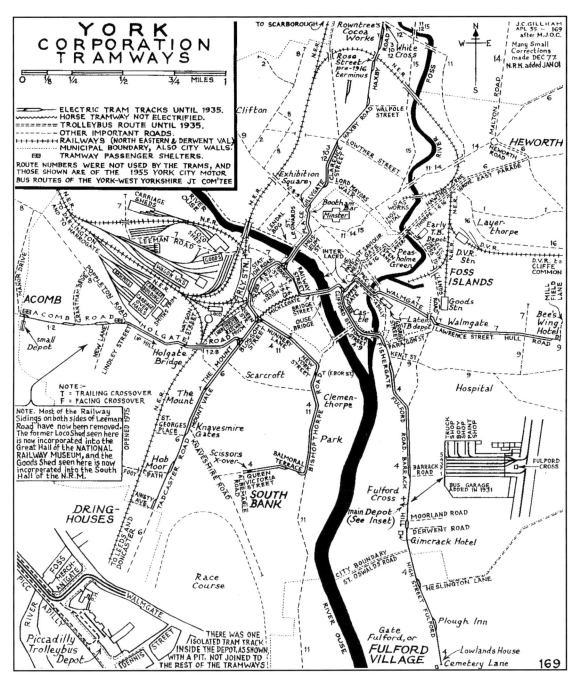

2. The York electric car system consisted of six radial routes spreading outwards from the NER Railway Station, a total route mileage of 8.5 miles. (J.C.Gillham)

3. The York Power Station which supplied electricity to the system was located on Foss Islands, alongside the river.

4. An interesting shot shows the tramlines being welded together by the Thermit process, which the Dick, Kerr contractors promised would provide 'a very smooth rail surface.'

OPENING DAY

5.   Civic dignitaries pose in front of decorated Car 1 on Clifford Street prior to the inaugural opening of the facility on 20th January 1910. The Mayor, Councillor James Birch, who drove the first vehicle, can be seen on the left, sporting his chain of office and flanked by his wife who exhibits the hauteur suitable for such an occasion. This view has been retouched by the photographer.

6.   A well loaded Car 1 poses on Clifford Street, whilst alternative modes of transport represented by the horses on the left register supreme indifference to the newcomer. Motorman J.A. Stewart stands on the mayor's right, presumably to prevent any unfortunate mishaps. Six trams took part in the procession, but only No.1 was decorated for the occasion.

7.   A close up of Car 1 features Mayor Birch as he fiddles unconvincingly with the controls. The well-dressed passengers were presumably councillors and other local bigwigs. The castle in the background was sadly pulled down in 1935, the same year that the system closed.

8.   Cars 1 and 2 pass the castle later the same day, inaugurating the Nessgate-Fulford service, with Motorman Stewart no longer in mufti. Car 2 boasts a full complement of riders, and carries the metal destination plates that endured until 1916. The clock tower of the police station looms behind the second tram, whilst the large dog on the left takes time to inspect the spanking new conveyances. The livery includes the Corporation crest visible on the rocker panel.

AROUND
THE STATION

9.   A view of the station yard, the hub of the whole network, has the imposing Station Hotel to the left and the medieval city walls on the right. Note the double track, with a third loop visible to the left of the rear tram, allowing three cars to stand side-by-side at busy times. Car 11 in the foreground, is bound for Dringhouses, and appears to have a driver under instruction on the front platform. Note the splendidly behatted ladies on the extreme right, making a real fashion statement.

10.   A later view of this busy venue, showing carts, carriages and motor vehicles awaiting passengers on the left. Car 36, visible under a line of bracket poles, was a 1916 series Brush tram. It came complete with vestibules and roller blinds, which show Haxby Road as the destination. The Station Hotel (centre) was built in 1887-88 and boasted 100 luxury rooms.

11.   A rare sight is of Car 37 at the station terminus around 1930. This vehicle, and No.38, was built at the York depot from one of the misconceived trailer cars, and utilised a long wheelbase truck salvaged from the 1910 water car. Note the lack of ventilator slots above the windows, due to the fact that the original saloon had a clerestory roof. Though the downstairs seating was longitudinal, the seats were leather upholstered. The livery, introduced in World War I, involved the removal of the lettering on the rocker panel. The tram behind is an early Brush example in its original state. No.37 is on the Fulford-Acomb run, its companion Haxby to South Bank.

12. Car 9, another unaltered vehicle, waits for the off to Acomb, sometime in the 1920s. The raised guard rails round the ends of the car were added in this decade as a precaution, after a dewiring trolleyboom struck an unfortunate passenger seated at the rear of the upper deck.

13. A good shot of one of the last additions to the fleet, car 42, which arrived from Burton-on-Trent in 1930. These cars originally boasted a covered top, and were mounted on 6ft wheelbase trucks. Note the angular dash panels and the good view of the elevated guard rails.

STATION ROAD

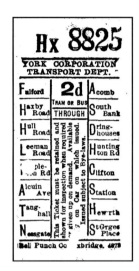

14.   This fine panoramic scene shows Car 26 of 1912 vintage, climbing onto Queen Street Bridge in vain pursuit of a Morris tourer which is keeping well clear of the tramlines. Note the row of taxis in the distance, whilst the building partly shadowed at the bottom right is the original York station of 1840.

15.   The Dick, Kerr workforce are here seen laying the tramlines on the Station Avenue curve leading to Rougier Street. The open field behind the railings was the exercise space for the animals from Walker's Horse Repository, and is now part of the Memorial Gardens.

→

16.   Taken from the opposite direction, this vista shows the twin tracks passing under the arch which was driven through the wall in 1874 to allow access to the station. Lendal Bridge is to the left and Rougier Street straight ahead. A 'Y' junction allowed trams from Lendal Bridge to either turn right under the arch into the station, or left towards the Ouse Bridge. The gentlemen posing on the right are presumably Dick, Kerr officials.

→

17.   A well-filled Car 2 passes behind the statue to George Leeman in Leeman Square on its way to Dringhouses via the station. Leeman (1809-82) was both Lord Mayor and MP for York, and Chairman of the NE Railway, and his statue was unveiled in 1885. It has since been moved a short distance north-west for traffic purposes.

18.   Car 14, having picked up a full complement of passengers from the station (note the sign above the platform entrance), rattles through the Station Road arch, and is about to cross the thoroughfare and enter Rougier Street en route to Fulford. Above the arch sightseers promenade along the medieval city walls.

19.   The tram visible on the right has just passed under the selfsame arch, but has turned left towards Lendal Bridge and Haxby. This postcard gives a good view of the walls on the left, whilst the towers of York Minster provide an imposing backdrop to the scene.

IN LOVING MEMORY

OF THE

York (Horse) Trams,

Which passed "peacefully" away

on Tuesday Evening Sept. 7th, 1909,

at 11-3 p.m.

GONE BUT NOT FORGOTTEN.

May they rest in pieces.

**Now we SHALL have to run, to run,
John Willie, Come on!**

20.   Work proceeds on laying the tramlines on Queen Street Bridge in the autumn and winter of 1909. In this scene, looking north-west along the line of the city walls, part of the station complex can be seen in the distance.

21.　　Two cars pause on the bridge with the Railway Institute on the right. Both vehicles are on a short-working to Lindley Street on the Acomb run. Car 35 is a 1916 class Brush tram, supplied with vestibules, and is here seen carrying the raised end guard rails. The picture gives a good view of the final 1931 livery of the cars, and shows some damage to the offside dash panel. Car 45 on the right, an ex-Burton example, was the last tram delivered to the undertaking.

22. This image of tracklaying along the south-eastern end of Queen Street shows well the sinuous course of the roadway as it heads towards the junction with Blossom Street in the far distance. The John Hunter Brewery sign at the top centre marks the position of the Windmill Hotel.

23. Brush Car 20 of 1912 vintage, is here seen turning out of Queen Street onto Blossom Street, probably on its way to Dringhouses. This tram was one of the few of the early conveyances to be retrospectively fitted with vestibules. Micklegate Bar is just out of sight on the right of the photograph.

FULFORD ROUTE
CLIFFORD STREET

24. The original plans for the horse car route involved the use of a double-deck steam tramcar designed by Edward Perrett. Two of these fearsome contraptions were tried out along the Fulford line in the autumn of 1880 but did not prove successful, mainly due to the opposition of locals along the route.

25. The city terminus of the Fulford horse trams was Nessgate/ Clifford Street where a group of company car crews can be seen gossiping behind one of the double-deckers, which is standing on the only stretch of double track on the whole line. The York Institute for Science, Art and Literature can be seen immediately to the right of the car, whilst on the extreme right is the Empire Theatre, now York Opera House.

TOWER STREET

26.   In 1909 operations on Castle Mills Bridge, which spanned the River Foss, were designed both to strengthen the structure and replace the old 4ft. gauge horse tram rails with a 3ft.6in. electric car track. A guardian of the law oversees the work, which must have caused massive short-term disruption to traffic as the nose-to-tail vehicles passing on the right suggest.

FISHERGATE

Journeyed Home — Sep. 7th, 1909.

R.I.P.

PASSENGERS LEFT BEHIND MAY GET THERE FIRST

TO BE BOTTLED 3 TRAM TAXS

PASSENGERS DESIRING TO SLEEP SHOULD INSTRUCT THE CONDUCTOR AT WHAT TIME THEY ARE TO BE AWAKENED

IN LOVING REMEMBRANCE

OF THE

Your (Horse) Trams,

Which ceased to exist at 11-5 p.m.

Tuesday, Sept. 7th, 1909,

GONE BUT NOT FORGOTTEN.

May they rest in pieces.

Now we SHALL have to run, to run.

John Willie, Come on!

27.   This comic card shows a horse car passing Fishergate Postern and was originally vended without the RIP overprint. Though caricaturing the decrepit state of the trams (as shown by the notices, and the passenger falling through the saloon floor) the depiction was not altogether wide of the mark!

28.   Another RIP card mourns the demise of the horse trams at 11.5pm on Tuesday, September 7th. 1909, though the York public seem to have been all too keen to get rid of them.

29.   A double-deck horse car passes rows of terraced shops as it negotiates one of the Fishergate turnouts, with the Light Horseman pub visible on the left in a locality which still preserves most of the buildings seen in this shot. Grange Garth leads off to the left in front of the inn.

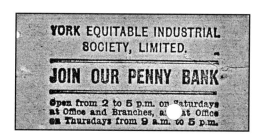

30.   Roller skating was all the rage in the early 20th century, and one of the electric cars is seen passing the City Roller Skating Palace with an appropriate audience for the photographer. Note the 'Maypole Dance' advertised for the 'Cinderella Carnival' on the posters. The rink later became the Rialto Cinema, and latterly a bingo hall.

FULFORD ROAD

31.   Car 2 is here seen heading north along Fulford Road, with Cemetery Road running off to the right. The building to the right of the tram is the local Conservative Club, fronted by a public convenience which is partly hidden by the foliage on the corner.

32.   A fine study of one of the well turned out horse cars in its chocolate and white livery posing for its picture outside the Imphal Infantry Barracks Armoury. The photograph picks out the fine detail of the double-decker, including the knifeboard seating on the open top.

33.   Another excellent shot, this time of Electric Car 4, on a pre-service trial judging by the motorman dressed in civvies, in January 1910. The picture was taken opposite the barracks, with the tram depot just off to the left. Again the image provides excellent detail of the car and its livery.

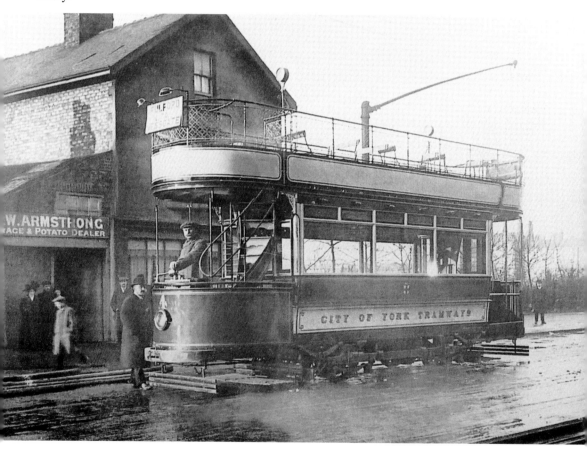

34.   The Fulford Cross tram depot is here shown in a picture taken in September 1911, probably on the same day as the group photograph of the crews shown in picture 93. Cars 11, 14, 4 and 16, all showing different destinations, parade in line abreast, manned by crews and inspectors. There are four tracks leading out of the tramshed, which merge into one. The single line then joins the main 'up' line heading for the city.

G   6432

YORK CORPORATION
TRAMWAYS & MOTORS

Fulford	2d THROUGH	Acomb
		South Bank
Hull Road		Dringhouses
Harby Road		Acomb
		South Bank
Newsgate		
Haxby Road		Dringhouses

This Ticket must be retained and shown for inspection when required or given up on demand. Available only on Car on which issued. Issued subject to Bye-laws.

MAIN STREET, FULFORD

35.   A horse tram plods up Main Street at a steady two miles per hour along a deserted thoroughfare, a completely different picture from today's thronged locality. On the centre left of the car is The Saddle hostelry.

36.   A well-patronised electric tram heads along the same roadway, with the spire of St Oswald's Church visible above the tram, a feature which has since been dismantled, whilst two lady cyclists head in the opposite direction. A finely-scrolled bracket arm pole carries the overhead, and again one is struck by the total absence of the local villagers.

37.   Another view of the same street, with Car 11 posed on the single line for the camera plus various locals ambling in shot. None would be so foolhardy as to hang about on the same road today, as it is now the busy A19. Note again the line of bracket poles supporting the running wire on the left.

38.   A splendid shot of Car 27 on the Fulford run, driven by a motorwoman (motorperson?) in this image taken circa 1916. The photograph shows clearly the main features of the Brush open-topper in its original livery. Note the oversized fleet number and the chain across the platform entrance. During the war the masked headlights of the York trams carried an illuminated cut-out letter for night identification of the route, in this case 'F' for Fulford.

← ——— 39. One of the horse cars stands by the Plough Inn, the terminus for these vehicles, already turned around for the return to Nessgate, with the patient beasts awaiting the signal for off. One wonders how much of an attraction the inn's 'Tea Gardens' represented for the local populace!

40. Another exemplary view of a spanking new Car 5 at the extended Fulford terminus, well-patronised by a full complement of riders including the top deck ladies with their oversized headgear. The attraction of these novel vehicles to the travelling public must have been considerable.

SOUTH BANK ROUTE

Qq 4759

YORK CORPORATION
TRANSPORT DEPT.

Fulford	2d	Acomb
Harby Road	TRAM OR BUS THROUGH	South Bank
Hull Road		Dring-houses
Leeman Road	This Ticket must be retained and shown for inspection when required or given up on demand. Available only on Car on which issued. Issued subject to Bye-laws.	Hunting-ton Rd
Poppleton Rd		Clifton
Alcuin Ave		Station
Tang-hall		Hewrth
Nessgate		StGrges Place

Bell Punch Co. Uxbridge. 4878

41.   Micklegate was the focus for several southerly tram routes, as cars approaching the triangular junction from Queen Street could either turn right for Acomb or Dringhouses, or straight ahead for South Bank. Here the junction lines for the electric trams are being laid in the autumn of 1909, with the Bar visible in the distance. Queen Street is on the left, and Nunnery Lane, starting point for the South Bank branch, runs off to the right. The Blossom Street track is at the bottom of the picture.

BISHOPTHORPE ROAD

42.   Images of the South Bank line are rare hence this view of the imposing edifice of Southlands Wesleyan Methodist Church at the corner of Southlands Road, built in 1886-87, will have to suffice. It does have the benefit of a fine scrolled bracket arm pole, with good detail of the running wire suspended on bowstrings, and the tramlines can be glimpsed at the bottom right-hand of the postcard.

QUEEN VICTORIA STREET

43.   Unfortunately the South Bank line was poorly served by local photographers during its lifetime, and this shot of Car 12 at the terminus is one of the few to emerge so far. The tram is pictured on the scissors crossover at the end of the terraced street, which, due to its proximity to the racecourse, would have been thronged with trams on race days. The post office on the right is on the corner of Albemarle Road. One interesting feature on the vehicle is the destination blind fixed above the motorman's head. They were soon repositioned above the top deck as they proved an obstacle to the taller drivers.

MICKLEGATE ROUTE

44.   The Micklegate branch was only ever used by the horse cars, and formed part of the line from Nessgate to The Mount. Electric trams could not pass through the narrow Micklegate Bar, and the route was abandoned along with the horse trams. Here a double-deck car approaches the Blossom Street turnout on the left, on its way to The Mount, having just emerged through the medieval gateway.

⟶

45.   This fine study of the Bar clearly shows the single track running through the gateway with an approaching horse tram framed in the entrance. Upper deck riders needed to remain sitting whilst the car passed through the gate.

PROVISIONAL ORDER.

BOARD OF TRADE.
SESSION 1881.

YORK TRAMWAYS.

(EXTENSIONS.)

NOTICE IS HEREBY GIVEN that application is intended to be made to the Board of Trade by the York Tramways Company (Limited) for a Provisional Order to authorise (among other things) the making, extending, and maintaining of Tramways in the City of York and County of the same City, and in the East Riding of the County of York, and to work such Tramways either by animal or mechanical power, and that certain of such Tramways are proposed to be laid along this street or road.

AND NOTICE IS HEREBY FURTHER GIVEN that notice of the application for a Provisional Order, containing a general description of the said Tramways and works, and such other particulars as are required to be given, will be published in this instant month of November in the "London Gazette." And that duplicate plans and sections, and a copy of the Gazette notice, will, on or before the 30th day of November instant, be deposited for public inspection with the Clerk of the Peace for the East Riding of the County of York, at his office in Beverley in the said East Riding, and also with the Clerk of the Peace for the City of York, and County of the same City, at his office at York, and that a copy of such plans and sections, together with a copy of the Gazette notice, will, on or before the said 30th day of November, be deposited at the office of the Board of Trade, Whitehall Gardens, and with the Town Clerk of the City of York, at his office at York ; and also that a copy of so much of the said plans and sections as relates to each of the parishes, townships, or extra parochial places from, in, through, or into which the proposed Tramways will be made or pass, together with a copy of the Gazette notice, will, on or before such 30th day of November instant, be deposited for public inspection with the Parish Clerk of each such parish at his place of abode, and in the case of an extra parochial place, with the Parish Clerk of some parish immediately adjoining thereto, at his place of abode.

Dated this 13th day of November, 1880.

BEST, WEBB & CO.,

6, Essex Street, Strand,

London, W.C.,

Solicitors and Parliamentary Agents for the Company.

46.   A horse car proceeds slowly up the steep line of Micklegate hill, just above the junction with George Hudson Street, assisted by the trace horse (incorrectly) attached to the vehicle. The last incumbent of this role was a wily quadruped called Dobbin, who knew the rules of his equine trade union to the letter. He willingly assisted his fellow beasts in dragging the tram uphill, but always halted at the top and speedily trotted back down the slope to his waiting nosebag!

47.   This supposedly humorous postcard shows the three horses hauling a car up the hill with St Martin-cum-Gregory Church in the background. Though the depiction of the state of the animals is in comic vein, the reality was not so far different from this cartoon. The poor beasts were routinely underfed and overworked, and their condition was a real blot on the escutcheon of those charged with their welfare.

DRINGHOUSES ROUTE

BLOSSOM STREET

48.   This fine and animated panorama shows an electric tram emerging from Queen Street with the destination board showing Dringhouses, which will involve a right turn into Blossom Street. Note the double track curving left, and the overhead, here supported on twin poles and span wire. The lady on the left pavement is pushing a sizeable pram, and in the distance the line of the old horse tram tracks can still be seen entering Micklegate Bar.

49.   Car 3 moves along Blossom Street on the straight one-mile run to Dringhouses. Note the metal destination plate, with the pair of lamps fixed above for night-time illumination.

THE MOUNT

50.   Car 14 picks up speed along the wide and open boulevard of The Mount. The gleaming condition of the tram and the lack of a destination plate suggest an early date in the life of the system. The running wire is here carried on twin poles and span wire.

51.   Views of single-deck horse cars are fairly singular, hence the interest in this example pictured on The Mount working the short-lived Nessgate – Station route. Note that the 16-seater is being pulled by a single horse.

52.   September 7th 1909 was the end of the horse trams and the last vehicle parades at The Mount terminus near Dalton Terrace. This was the practical limit of horse operation as Mount Vale to the south had a 1 in 22 gradient, no obstacle to electric trams but impossible for animal power. Behind the trees is Driffield Terrace, site of a considerable Romano-British cemetery sited alongside the old Roman road leading into York which lies under the present A1036.

MOUNT VALE

53.   Car 10 pauses at Mount Vale before running off the double track onto the single line by St George's Place visible on the left. Knavesmire Road heads off to the right of the picture. Note how the road behind the tram climbs northward to the city, and the overhead cables feeding power to the running wire.

TADCASTER ROAD

54.   Car 11 stands at Dringhouses terminus with Ainsty Avenue on the left and the racecourse on the right. The tram is parked just in front of the bifurcation of the terminal length of track, which allowed two cars to park side-by-side.

ACOMB ROUTE

HOLGATE ROAD

55.   This view shows the layout of the 'Y' junction leading from Holgate Road in the foreground into Blossom Street which crosses from left to right. Note the various paraphernalia scattered about, and the police constable checking operations as he stands at the entrance to East Mount Road.

56.   This panorama of Blossom Street looks north-east, with Micklegate Bar hidden in the distant haze. On the left the 'Y' junction swings west into Holgate Road. The picture suggests a scene of utter chaos, and one wonders just how road traffic coped whilst the tramlines were being laid. A ghost figure lingers by the standard on the left, victim of the long exposures then necessary to secure good images.

57.   Car 10 climbs westward up the winding length of Holgate Hill under running wire supported on side-arm poles. The lack of a destination board suggests that the image was taken when Holgate Bridge was being rebuilt and the service was a shuttle one. The sails of Acomb windmill can be seen above the trolleyboom of the tram.

58.   At the foot of the hill Car 17 proceeds west towards Acomb. On this part of the route twin posts and span wire carry the overhead as far as the terminus. Note the military-looking equestrian figure, with others riding behind the tram.

ACOMB ROAD

59.   Car 10 approaches the Acomb Road, Poppleton Road and Holgate Road junctions, a postwar shot judging by the indicator board on the tram which is now sited above the top deck. Note the neat passenger shelter on the right of the photograph.

60.   Acomb terminus, and a schoolboy scuttles away home clutching his satchel, as other riders load and unload from Car 10 in a more leisurely fashion. The tram pole on the right looks decidedly unsteady! Somewhere behind it lay the temporary tramshed which housed two cars stationed there to service the shuttle run to Holgate Bridge, before the structure was strengthened.

HAXBY ROAD ROUTE

LENDAL BRIDGE

61.   Two shots which show Lendal Bridge being strengthened for tramcar operation. In this vista the bridge has been stripped before girder replacement and reconstruction. Note the lifebelts hanging on the bridge rails, presumably placed there to aid unfortunates who insisted on falling into the Ouse!

Ma 5154

City of York Tramways

1d

2

CHILD'S TICKET

This Ticket is issued subject to the Bye-laws & Regulations of the Corporation, to be retained for inspection and given on demand.

62.   At a slightly later date Car 16 edges gingerly along the bridge, running 'wrong line' on the single track then completed. On the right the second line approaches completion as girders and pipework are sorted out under the inspection of a bowler-hatted foreman.

64.   Car 11, one of the few early fleet vehicles to be vestibuled, crosses the bridge on its way to Acomb in 1933.

63.   Car 6 heads for Haxby over the rebuilt bridge, ignominiously passed by a coal cart! The imposing structure on the left is one of the city's original water supply towers.

MUSEUM STREET

65.   Several versions of this 1930s scene ⟶
exist. Here Car 14, in its unaltered state, pauses
for its picture on its way to South Bank. It is
about to be passed by a Tilling-Stevens single
deck petrol bus arriving from Haxby. In another
shot the gentleman here seen climbing into his
motorcar is shown cranking up the vehicle's
engine.

66.   Over 20 years earlier Car 8 stops by the
entrance to the Museum Gardens on the left in
sylvan surroundings. The City Library is hidden
by the trees behind the tram, which is on a short-
working from the railway station to Haxby.
Alternative forms of transport can be seen lined
up on the right of the car.

⟶
67.   A fine shot of the north-east end of the street with the Minster looming up behind Car 18,
which is halted by Thomas's Hotel on its way to the station. The tower on the left belongs to St
Wilfrid's Catholic Church.

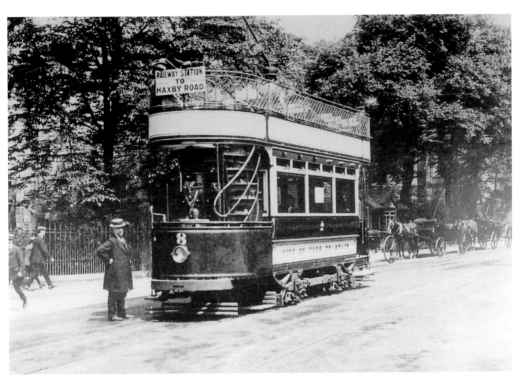

68.   Car 3 swings left into St Leonard's Place, pursued by a Hansom cab. The building visible behind the trolleyboom is the Red House, erected in 1714 by Sir William Robinson, a former mayor and MP. It is now an antiques centre.

Three vignettes of York electric tramway personalities.

Mr. J. W. Hame,
Chief Electrical Engineer and Tramways Manager.

Alderman R. H. V. Wragge.
Chairman, Tramways Committee, York.

Mr. F. W. Spurr,
City Engineer, York.

69.   Car 31, a vestibuled 1913 Brush model, stops outside the fine crescent which is now home to the offices of York City Council. The artillery piece on the right was situated on land outside the Territorial Army office which is now a car park. A stately open-top automobile sails past on the left, whilst a postman trundles his delivery trolley on the opposite side of the road.

70.   An early image of Car 8 shows it passing Exhibition Square on the left, the home of York Art Gallery. The lack of a destination board suggests the tram was short-working to Lendal Bridge whilst it was undergoing strengthening.

71.   Taken from the opposite decoration, this excellent panorama from a 1912 postcard shows an electric tram on its way to the station, with upper-deck ladies using parasols to shield their complexions from the sun. Bootham Bar, built on the site of the Roman fortress gate, can be seen on the left, with the towers of the Minster rising behind.

CITY OF YORK.

YORK CORPORATION BILL, 1902.

POLL OF OWNERS AND RATEPAYERS.

EXPLANATION OF RESOLUTIONS.

No. 1. The effect of this Resolution is to Confirm a contract made on the 29th January, 1901, between the City of York Tramways Co., Ltd., and the York Corporation for the **purchase** by the latter of the **existing Tramways** in the City and Fulford, and the **Freehold Depot** in Fulford Road containing **1,538 superficial yards.**

GILLYGATE

72.   Car 8 crosses from Gillygate into St Leonard's Square, travelling wrong line as it comes off the single track onto double. It has no indicator board so it may be on the short-working from Lendal Bridge to Haxby whilst the bridge was being strengthened in mid-1910.

The price to be paid for the Tramway Undertaking, including the lines and the Freehold Depot in Fulford Road, is £12,000.

The Cars, Horses, &c., are to be paid for at a valuation.

If the Tramways are purchased, **the Corporation will be able to keep the Roadway and Tram Lines in efficient repair, and work,** let or lease the running of Tram Cars **by Horses** until it is considered desirable to adopt a more modern and economical system of traction.

The Bill provides in Clause 35 thereof for the running of a **sufficient service of carriages for Artisans, Mechanics and daily Labourers at Cheap Fares** on going to or returning from their daily work.

No. 2.   The Council seek powers to extend the existing line on the Mount as far as St. George's Place, to make additional passing places on the existing lines, and to put down tram lines from the Haxby Road and Clifton districts, past the Railway Station and up Holgate Road as far as the Fox Inn.

73.   A comparatively quiet Gillygate is a complete change from the nose-to-tail traffic now encountered there during most of the day. Here Car 14, on a short-working to Lendal Bridge, takes the single line linking it to Clarence Street. The frontages are much as they remain to this day, whilst the hound at the bottom left is obviously doing a spot of shopping.

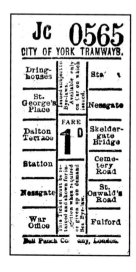

Jc 0565
CITY OF YORK TRAMWAYS.

Dring-houses	Issued subject to Bye-laws. Available only on Car on which issued.	Sta'
St. George's Place		Nessgate
Dalton Terrace	FARE 1 0	Skelder-gate Bridge
Station		Ceme-tery Road
Nessgate	This Ticket must be re-tained and shown for in-spection when required or given up on demand See Bye-law.	St. Oswald's Road
War Office		Fulford

Bell Punch Company, London.

CLARENCE STREET

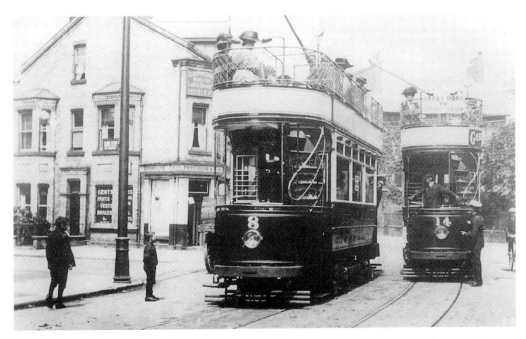

74.   This study was taken at the junction between Gillygate, Clarence Street, Claremont Terrace (to the left), and Lord Mayor's Walk on the right. It shows an incident usually frowned upon by tramway management, as the crews of Cars 8 and 14 engage in chit-chat witnessed by the top deck ladies in their headdress finery.

75.   An empty-looking Car 8 heads for Haxby following the double line north-east, the running wire mounted on left-hand bracket poles, with Union Terrace off to the left.

HAXBY ROAD

76.   Car 24 is here seen just north of the junction with Wigginton Road, with Clarence Gardens visible on the left.

→

77.   Taken from the opposite direction, Car 14 heads for Haxby with Clarence Gardens this time on the right of the shot. The tram is moving onto the loop, with Walpole Street on the immediate left.

→

78.   Nearing journey's end, Car 8 passes the entrance to the vicarage and the junction with Rose Street, both on the right. The City Hospital is behind the trees on the left.

79.   Car 14 rests at the pre-1916 terminus on Haxby Road with the vicarage gate in shot at the bottom left of the photograph. In early 1916 the tracks were extended over the NER bridge on the right for the convenience of the Rowntree's workforce.

80.   The post-1916 Haxby terminus shows unreconstructed Brush Car 1 waiting on the terminal loop, whilst the crew relax in the saloon in this 1920s image. The view is looking south down Haxby Road, and the trolleyboom has not yet been swung for the return journey to Acomb. The Tilling-Stevens motorbus in the distance was probably running in competition with the tram, ferrying Rowntree's workers back into the city.

HULL ROAD ROUTE

ROUGIER STREET

81.   A rather dilapidated looking Car 16 is here pictured running north-west along Rougier Street on its return from Hull Road in 1933. It is passing Lumb's Newsagents on the corner of Rougier Street and Station Road. Note the destination board in the centre saloon window of the vehicle. The posters above the tram extol the benefits both of Ovaltine and a visit to Blackpool!

Fp 8216		
CITY OF YORK TRAMWAYS		
Fulford	Ordin<ry> Fare	eslington Lane
Infantry Barracks	1½d	Grange Street
Skeldergate Bridge		Nessgate
Tanner Row		Stat:
Holgate Corner		Watson Street
Acomb		Lindley Street
Lowther Street		Haxby Road
Victoria Bar		Museum Street
South Bank Avenue		Bewlay Street
Dring- houses		South Bank
James Street		St.Georges Place
Bull Punch Co., Uxbridge. 2·24		Hull Road

BRIDGE STREET

82.	Chaos reigns supreme along the western approach to Ouse Bridge as a horse car derails with a broken axle, with a following vehicle trapped behind. The building on the left is Boyes Department Store, which was burned down in 1910. The usual mass of idlers has speedily appeared to observe others' misfortunes!

83.	At the same place some years later the store can be seen after rebuilding. Car 3, in its 1910 condition, rattles its way to Hull Road. Coming from the opposite direction is well-filled vestibuled tram No.31. Note the car stop sign on the right-hand stanchion, one of a pair of twin poles supporting the overhead at this point.

84.	In this photograph taken from the other side of the bridge, cyclists and pedestrians negotiate the river crossing, whilst vestibuled Car 36 takes its passengers to the racecourse. Note the splendidly rebuilt Boyes premises with riverside views available to the patrons of its café.

LOW OUSEGATE

85.   Heading east across Ouse Bridge the tramway entered Ousegate, and took a sharp right-hand bend into Nessgate, passing St Michael's Church on the left. This photograph shows the acuteness of the turn taken by the twin track. The tower of the church was removed in the 1960s when it became unsafe.

86.   A good view of double-deck Horse Tram 5 waiting at the Nessgate terminus alongside the Empire Theatre, whose doorway can be glimpsed above the horses. The underframe of the car is inscribed 'CITY OF YORK TRAMWAYS. W. CHIPPER, MANAGER' in tiny letters. Note the variety of national advertisements displayed on the decency boards attached to the upper deck guard rails.

PICCADILLY

87.   Hull Road trams travelled along Coppergate and swung right into Piccadilly. In this photograph the twin lines are curving left into the short stretch of Merchant Gate before turning right onto Walmgate. This 1935 picture gives a good view of the twin poles and span wire carrying the overhead, complete with frogs, as it sweeps around the bend. The pub on the right-hand corner is the Red Lion.

WALMGATE

88.   Car 3 grinds along Walmgate under running wire carried on bracket poles, as it heads towards the city centre. The lady at the bottom right seems to be wearing an immoderately short skirt for the early 1930s when this scene was taken!

Ticket issued 16.11.1935

89.   An all-female crew pose at the Hull Road terminus in Car 17, probably in 1916 when
women were recruited both for driving and conducting duties. The tram is still in its original
condition, before the removal of the lettering on the rocker panel and the replacement of the metal
indicator board with roller blinds. The stencil letter in the dashlight is 'H'.

90.   Car 8 appears at the same venue, alongside the quaintly-named Bee's Wing Hotel. The photograph is post-1916, when the dash panel lost its lettering and roller blinds replaced the old metal plates. The blinds were soon moved from their position above the motormen's heads, as they tended to obstruct taller drivers like the one on the left.

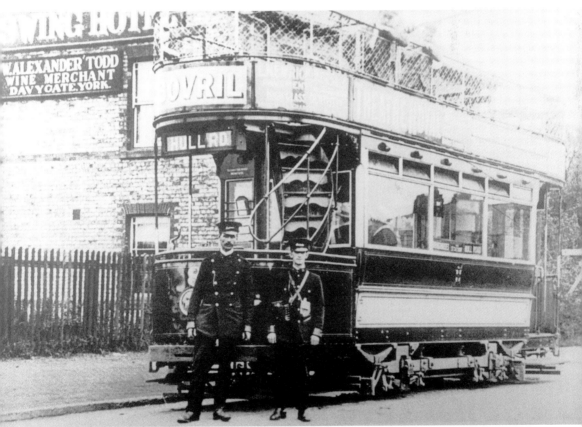

CARS AND CREWS

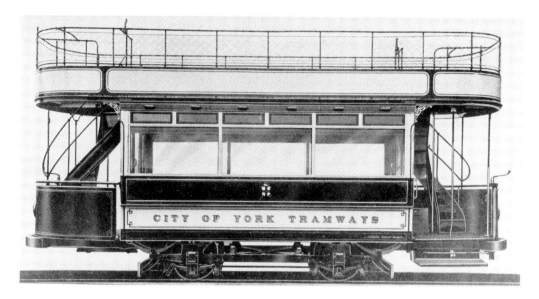

91.   An excellent side elevation of one of the original 1910 Brush open-toppers before receiving its electrics and trolleyboom. Note particularly the 8ft. 6in. long wheelbase truck then being manufactured by the company in their efforts to produce a successful flexible four-wheel underframe.

92.   No images of York Water Car 19 appear to have survived, but the vehicle was identical to one produced for the Chesterfield system in 1909, apart from the fact that the York vehicle was constructed to run on narrow gauge track. The Derbyshire example is here seen at the Brush works prior to delivery.

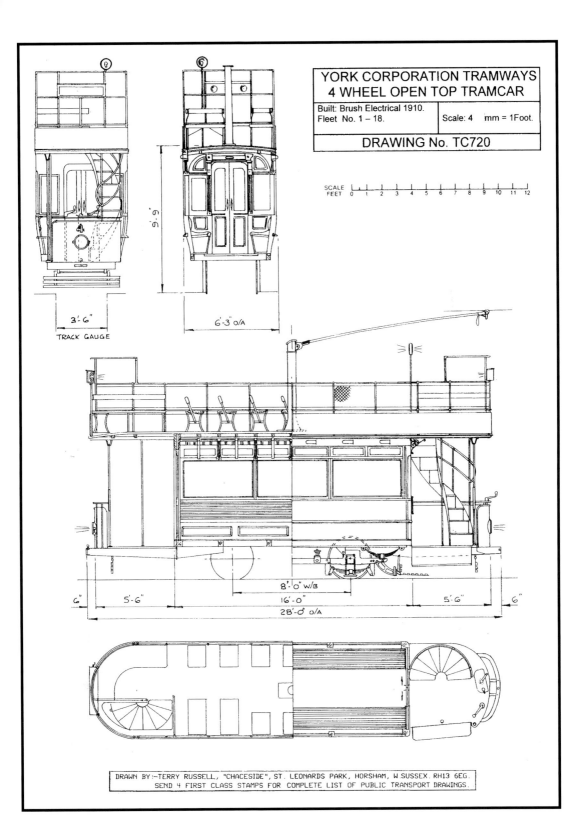

YORK CORPORATION TRAMWAYS
4 WHEEL OPEN TOP TRAMCAR

Built: Brush Electrical 1910.
Fleet No. 1 – 18.

Scale: 4 mm = 1Foot.

DRAWING No. TC720

SCALE FEET 0 1 2 3 4 5 6 7 8 9 10 11 12

3'-6"
TRACK GAUGE

9'-6"

6'-3 o/A

8'-0" w/B

16'-0"

28'-0 o/A

6" 5'-6" 5'-6" 6"

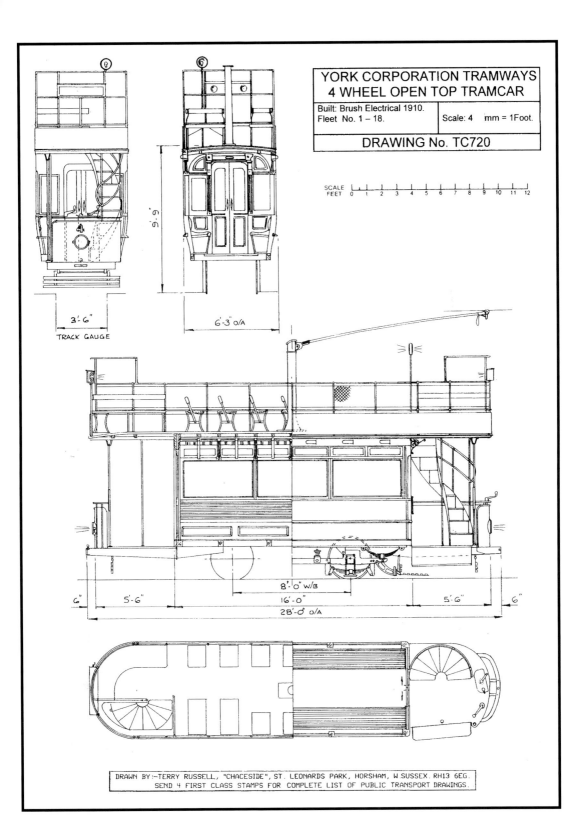

DRAWN BY:-TERRY RUSSELL, "CHACESIDE", ST. LEONARDS PARK, HORSHAM, W.SUSSEX. RH13 6EG.
SEND 4 FIRST CLASS STAMPS FOR COMPLETE LIST OF PUBLIC TRANSPORT DRAWINGS.

93.　Car crews parade for posterity at the Fulford Cross Depot in September 1911. The straw-hatted gent is the traffic manager, Walter Chipper, whilst the top-hatted figure on his right is the manager J.W. Hame.

Ticket issued 16.11.1935

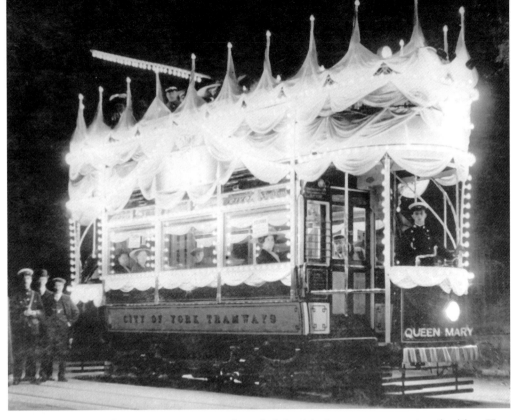

94, 95. Decorating fleet trams was an art form indulged in by most transport authorities. Here are two views of Car 22 appropriately decorated and lit up for the Coronation of George V on June 22nd 1911. At one end is the name of the monarch's wife, whilst his presumably graces the opposite dash panel.

96.   A fine body of York conductresses, exuding a military-style demeanour that would probably have struck fear into the Huns had they ever confronted them. They are equipped with workmanlike coats and hats and look a thoroughly capable band.

⟶

97.   Car 6 at Dringhouses terminus, with 'D' clearly displayed in the masked headlamp. The mixed crew includes a 'civvy' on the platform, presumably a lady driver under instruction. One wonders whatever happened to 'P & O Chutney – the King of Sauces'?

Um 6569

YORK CORPORATION
TRANSPORT DEPT.

Fulford	**2d**	Acomb
Haxby Road	TRAM	South Bank
Hull Road	THROUGH	Dring-houses
Leeman Road		Hunting ton Rd
Popple-ton Rd		Clifton
Alcuin Ave		Station
Tang-hall		Hew'rth
Ness-gate		St Grgo's Place
Williamson		nter. Ashton

Ticket issued 16.11.1935

98.   Car 21 at Hull Road boasts a capable-looking female crew ready
for the off. The sign behind the conductress warns that riding on the steps,
platforms and stairs is strictly prohibited.

99.   Another mixed crew at Acomb work Tram 27, displaying its oversized fleet number. A summer date is suggested by the motorman's white-topped cap.

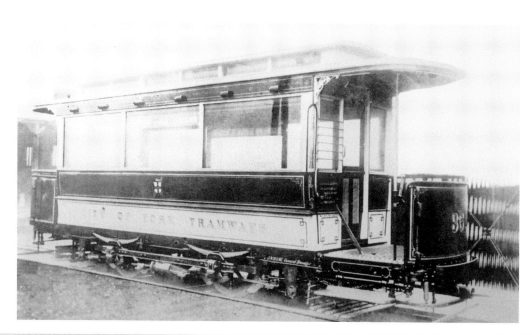

100.   Trailer cars, such as No.35 shown here, one of a batch of four 22-seaters, were never a good idea, and were soon consigned to the back of the depot. Two of these misconceived contrivances were later converted into electric vehicles at the Fulford premises.

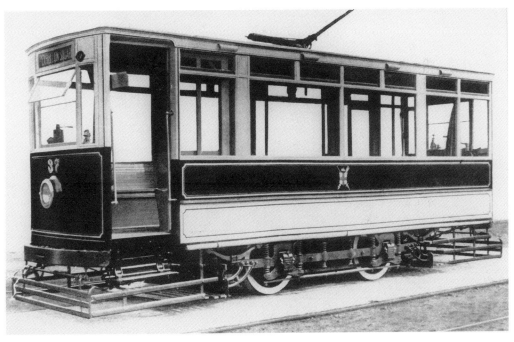

101.   One of the trailers is seen here connected to Car 2, presumably on an initial trial. Unfortunately the 25hp motors of the earlier Brush vehicles were not strong enough to haul a fully-laden tram and trailer, and they had to await the arrival of the 1916 class trams with their more potent power units.

102.   An ex-works view of English Electric front-entrance demi-car 37 of 1925 vintage. The advanced-looking vehicle was a single-deck one-man tram with electrically-operated doors and a 6ft. wheelbase, and was scheduled for the Dringhouses – Hull Road route, but two accidents, one in thick fog, lessened public appeal for it, and it ended life ignominiously as a salt/sand conveyer.

103. The rather spartan interior of the 24-seater was at variance with its smart modern exterior appearance. Note the hard wooden seating and the dividing partitions. The hanging straps show that a proportion of the riders were expected to stand.

——————→

104. The end of it all, as at midnight on 16th November 1935, Car 1 led a procession of four vehicles from Nessgate to the depot. Mayor W.H. Shaw handles the controls under the expert eye of Inspector J.A. Stewart on his right, nearly 25 years after the latter assisted Mayor Birch to drive the selfsame tram at the very start of the service.

Oa 9749

YORK CORPORATION and
WEST YORKSHIRE R.C.
Co. Ltd. - JOINT SERVICES
Dog or Luggage Ticket

| Inward | FARE | Inward |
| Outward | 1d | Outward |

Accepted solely at Passengers Risk

LUGGAGE

This Ticket must be retained and shown if required for our service.

DOGS

Not allowed on the seats of the tramcars and to be kept under proper control

Williamson, Printer, Ashton

Ticket issued 16.11.1935

TROLLEYBUSES

105.   In 1914, the corporation ordered four battery-powered buses from the Edison Electric Company. The little 24-seaters went into service between Heworth and Clifton, and were one-man operated. Here No.3 (DN-12) is shown off at the commencement of their short lives. Note the deep lifeguards which prevented pedestrians from falling under the vehicles.

106.   The battery buses were worn out by 1919 and a trackless route was substituted between the city and Heworth to the north-east. It was operated with four Railless front-entrance 24-seat single-deckers (DN2985-8), numbered 6-9 which were later reduced to 20-seaters. All these vehicles were withdrawn by the end of 1929. The photograph shows a manufacturer's impression of one of the boxy single-deckers.

107.   The corporation decided to reactivate the trolleybus line in early 1931, and borrowed a double-deck demonstrator from Doncaster (DT2168, No.22) to test out the route. This image shows one of the three-axle Karrier-Clough E6 60-seaters identical to the vehicle which carried out the trials.

HEWORTH ROUTE

FULFORD CROSS DEPOT

108.   The photograph shows the three cutting-edge single-deck 32-seat Karrier-Clough E4s which were used to service the reopened line. Bearing registration numbers VY2291-3 and numbered 30-32, they were up-to-date streamlined vehicles in a very pleasing blue and white colour scheme similar to that gracing the contemporary tramcars. They are here seen displayed, trolleys down, in front of the extended depot. No special wiring was provided to take them onto the roadway; they used the positive tram wire, and a skate trailing in the tramline.

109.   Karriers 30, 31 and 32 are here seen lined-up inside the depot at the start of their operational service.

PAVEMENT

110.   The three Karriers used single-line wiring from the depot to take them to the city terminus at Pavement. Here Karrier 32 runs through the terminus loop on its way to the stop. The picture gives an excellent view of the rear of these buses, and the turning circle above. Note that the span wire carrying the overhead is here fixed to rosettes mounted on the street walls.

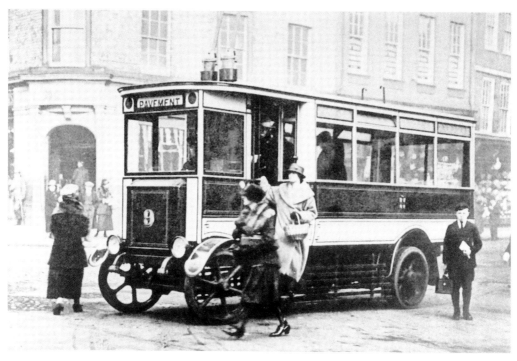

111. Railless 9 halts at the terminus, offloading a pair of fashionable-looking ladies, whilst the schoolboy on the right poses for his picture. Parliament Street is immediately behind the primitive-looking bus. A comparison with the Karriers shows how far trackless design had progressed in the eleven years between the building of the two sets of buses.

112. One of the Railless trolleybuses negotiates the Pavement loop as it manoeuvres to pick up passengers. One advantage the trolleybuses held over the trams was their ability to come close to the kerb.

WHIP-MA-WHOP-MA GATE

113.   This weirdly-named street is the shortest thoroughfare in York, albeit with the longest name. Here Karrier 30, pursued by a double-deck motorbus, heads towards St Saviourgate on its way to Heworth.

LAYERTHORPE

114.   Photographs of the short-lived Heworth railless route are of necessity scarce, but this photograph, taken from Peasholme Green, shows Layerthorpe Bridge just before its widening in 1925. Twin poles and span wire carry the overhead above the decidedly narrow bridge and give way to bracket poles on the far side. After widening the twin sets of running wire were set further apart. The long, flat-roofed building on the right is the York County Laundry.

EAST PARADE

115.   Railless 9 is here seen running towards the city along a routeway lined by terraced houses distinguished by a variety of designs. The overhead is here suspended from bracket poles bereft of any fancy wrought iron scrolling.

E   1599
CITY OF YORK TRAMWAYS
Fare - 3d

NESSGATE to KNAVESMIRE GATES

KNAVESMIRE GATES to NESSGATE

This ticket is available for one journey only and is issued subject to the Bye-laws and Regulations of the Corporation. The Conductor is required to punch the ticket in the section for which it is issued, and it must be produced or delivered up by the passenger on demand for inspection.

116.   Heading in the opposite direction, Karrier 30 is the centrepiece of a fine study of trolleybus operation, as the vehicle passes Second Avenue on the left under a line of bracket poles. Note the 'CARS STOP BY REQUEST' sign on the left-hand standard, and the iron railings on the right, once a feature of English towns. Most of these perished in wartime scrap drives.

117.   At the north-eastern end of East Parade Railless 9 turns right off Heworth Road as passengers embark riskily from the roadway, though the stop sign is by the pavement on the far right. The imposing turreted spire in the background belongs to Heworth Methodist Chapel, built in 1890.

118.   An unknown photographer has produced a fine study of Karrier 31 heading for York along a deserted country lane bounded by trees and running under bracket poles. The city coat-of-arms stands out well on the front panel and forms part of a very tasteful livery. The 19 ft. trolleybooms could swing 13 ft. to either side of the trackless to enable it to bypass obstacles.

HEWORTH
TERMINUS

119.   Journey's end as one of the Railless cars parks by the well-built bus shelter under the turning circle. Malton Road is just behind the squared-off rear of the trackless, whilst Stockton Lane leads off to the right.

120.   Karrier 30 shows off its profile at the same tree-lined venue, a shot which also gives a good view of the turning loop above. Unlike the Railless cars, the Karriers had the services of a conductor, here pictured standing in the wide rear entrance of the bus.

THE
YORK TRAMWAYS COMPANY,
LIMITED.

Capital £14,000, in 5 per cent. Cumulative Preference Shares £10 each.

And £13,240 in Ordinary Shares £10 each.

DIRECTORS.

FRANCIS J HESELTINE, Esq.
Director of the Derby and Gothenburg Tramways Co.'s.

ALDERMAN W. W. WILBERFORCE,
Ex Lord Mayor of York.

EVERITT EVERITT, Esq.,
Director of the Manchester, Bury, Rochdale, and Oldham Tramways Company.

BANKERS.

THE YORK CITY AND COUNTY BANK, YORK.

SOLICITORS.

Messrs. LEEMAN, WILKINSON & CO., York.
Messrs. BEST, WEBB & TEMPLETON, Essex Street, London.

ENGINEER.

JOSEPH KINCAID, Esq., M. Inst., C.E.

SECRETARY.

FRANKLIN HURST, Esq., Nessgate, York, and 11, Great George Street, Westminster, S.W.

SALE BY PRIVATE TENDER

OF

400 5°/₀ Preference £10 Shares, at £10 each,

AND

400 Fully Paid Ordinary £10 Shares, at £7 10 each.

Messrs. HODSON & COPPOCK, Stock Brokers, Commercial Buildings, Manchester, are prepared to receive Tenders for the whole or any portion of these Shares. No Tender will be received for a smaller number than 5 Shares, nor at a less sum than the minimum prices above stated.

The first section of the Tramways which has been worked by the Company for some months past is two miles in length, and traverses the districts of York and suburbs. The traffic on this section is carried on principally by one horse Cars, giving a well known advantage in economical working.

MP **Middleton Press**

EVOLVING THE ULTIMATE RAIL ENCYCLOPEDIA

Easebourne Lane, Midhurst, West Sussex.
GU29 9AZ   Tel:01730 813169

www.middletonpress.co.uk   email:info@middletonpress.co.uk

A-0 906520   B-1 873793   C-1 901706   D-1 904474

OOP Out of Print at time of printing - Please check current availability   **BROCHURE AVAILABLE SHOWING NEW TITLES**